The Civil War Begins

Jane H. Gould

CRABTREE
Publishing Company
www.crabtreebooks.com

UNDERSTANDING THE CIVIL WAR

Author: Jane H. Gould
Publishing plan research and development:
  Sean Charlebois, Reagan Miller
  Crabtree Publishing Company
Editors: Mark Cheatham, Kirsten Holm, Lynn Peppas
Proofreader: Wendy Scavuzzo
Editorial director: Kathy Middleton
Production coordinator: Shivi Sharma
Creative director: Arka Roy Chaudhary
Design: Sandy Kent
Cover design: Samara Parent
Photo research: Iti Shrotriya
Maps: Paul Brinkdopke
Production coordinator: Margaret Amy Salter
Prepress technician: Margaret Amy Salter
Print coordinator: Katherine Berti

Written, developed, and produced by Planman Technologies

Photographs and Reproductions
Front cover: © CORBIS; Title Page (p. 1): Library of Congress; Table of Contents (p. 3): Chapter 1: Library of Congress (left), Ken Welsh/Photolibrary (right); Chapter 2: Library of Congress; Chapter 3: Library of Congress; Chapter 4: Bettmann/CORBIS; Chapter 5: North Wind / North Wind Picture Archives. Chapter Opener image (pp. 5, 13, 23, 31): Library of Congress
Corbis: p. 38 (bottom); Bettmann: p. 37; Mathew B. Brady: p. 18; Eon Images: p. 19; Library of Congress: pp. 7, 10, 11 (top and bottom); pp. 21, 22 (top and bottom), pp. 25, 27, 29, 33, 35, 38 (top), 40, 42; North Wind Picture Archives: pp. 4, 16, 44; Photolibrary: Ken Welsh, p. 9.

Front cover: An illustration shows the attack on Fort Sumter.
Back cover (background): A military map of the United States from 1862 shows forts and military posts.
Back cover (logo): A civil war era cannon stands in front of the flag from Fort Sumter.
Title page (top): The shelling of Fort Sumter by the South Carolina militia signaled the beginning of the Civil War.
Title page (bottom): The guns at Fort Sumter returned fire at the South Carolina militia.

Library and Archives Canada Cataloguing in Publication

Gould, Jane H., 1956-
    The Civil War begins / Jane H. Gould.

(Understanding the Civil War)
Includes index.
Issued also in electronic formats.
ISBN 978-0-7787-5338-4 (bound).--ISBN 978-0-7787-5355-1 (pbk.)

    1. United States--History--Civil War, 1861-1865--Campaigns--Juvenile literature. I. Title. II. Series: Understanding the Civil War

E470.G68 2011   j973.7'3   C2011-907490-7

Library of Congress Cataloging-in-Publication Data

CIP available at Library of Congress

Crabtree Publishing Company

www.crabtreebooks.com   1-800-387-7650

Printed in the U.S.A./112011/JA20111018

Published in Canada
Crabtree Publishing
616 Welland Ave.
St. Catharines, Ontario
L2M 5V6

Published in the United States
Crabtree Publishing
PMB 59051
350 Fifth Avenue, 59th Floor
New York, New York 10118

Published in the United Kingdom
Crabtree Publishing
Maritime House
Basin Road North, Hove
BN41 1WR

Published in Australia
Crabtree Publishing
3 Charles Street
Coburg North
VIC 3058

TABLE *of* CONTENTS

> *Our Southern brethren have done grievously, they have rebelled and have attacked their father's house and their loyal brothers. They must be punished and brought back, but this necessity breaks my heart.*
>
> --Major Robert Anderson, Union commander at Fort Sumter

Citizens of Charleston watching Fort Sumter under attack in Charleston Harbor, South Carolina, April 12, 1861.

Crisis at Fort Sumter!

I n 1776, America's 13 colonies broke from England and formed the United States. In less than 100 years, disagreements between the North and South started to break the **Union** apart. The people in these areas shared a common language and history. By 1860, though, they began to think their differences could not be overcome.

Causes of the Civil War

The main cause of this split between the North and South was **slavery**. Many people in the Southern states believed slavery was necessary. Without it, they could not grow cotton, and cotton was important for their **economy**.

Many Southerners believed that each state should decide on its own laws. Southerners did not think the **federal government** in Washington, DC, should tell them what to do.

The economies of the North and South were very different. The North had a greater population, more miles of railroads, and more industry. Its farms produced more food. The economy of the South was heavily dependent on one crop—cotton.

Many Northerners wanted the government to end slavery. Regardless of what they thought about slavery, most people wanted the South to stay in the Union.

Major Events

1857

March
Dred Scott decision

1859

October
John Brown raids
Harper's Ferry,
Virginia

1860

November
Lincoln elected
president

1861

April
South Carolina
militia fires on
Fort Sumter

What Do You Know!

SLAVE POPULATION
In 1860, there were close to four million slaves in the United States. That means almost one out of every eight people was a slave.

The Road to War

From 1850 to 1860, relations worsened between people who were anti-slavery (against slavery) and pro-slavery (for slavery). People called **abolitionists** were against slavery. They worked to pass laws to end slavery, but there were many people in the government who supported it.

The Western Territories

By 1850, America had added territories in the West all the way to California. Soon the question of slavery came up. Should these territories allow slavery or not? If a federal law said these were free territories, with no slaves, the Southern states would lose power in Congress.

Many Southerners were afraid that the North would gain control of the government. The abolitionists would have their way. In 1856, violence broke out in the western territory of Kansas and soon spread to the East.

Dred Scott

Emotions got even stronger in 1857. Dred Scott was an enslaved person who traveled and lived with his master in free states, where slavery was illegal. They later traveled back to states where slavery was still legal. When his master died, Scott tried to buy his freedom but was refused. He took his case to court and claimed that he was no longer a slave. The **U.S. Supreme Court** said that because Scott was a slave, he was not a citizen. Therefore, he could not bring his case to court. The Supreme Court also said that neither the U.S. government nor a territory had the right to stop slavery. The South saw this decision as a great victory. Many Northerners were angry. Even people who were not abolitionists began to change their minds.

> *I, John Brown, am now quite certain that the crimes of this guilty land will never be purged away but with Blood.*
>
> —The last letter of John Brown before he was hanged, December 2, 1859

John Brown

In 1859, the trouble that started in Kansas reached a peak in Virginia. An abolitionist named John Brown decided that only violence would end slavery. He wanted to start an **uprising** of slaves against their masters. Brown and a group of 18 men captured an **arsenal** of weapons at Harper's Ferry that belonged to the U.S. government. They took **hostages** and

people were killed. The U.S. Marines attacked Brown and his men
and captured them. Brown was hanged. The South called Brown
a murderer. Many abolitionists, however, thought he was a hero.
People on both sides worked themselves into a raging anger.

Abraham Lincoln's Election

Abraham Lincoln, a Republican, was elected president in
1860. Politics were so divided that the South voted almost
solidly for the Democratic Party and the North voted
Republican. Lincoln won the election without winning
one Southern state. Lincoln's victory showed the South
that it had lost political power.

   Lincoln did not want to upset Southerners. He said that
the government would not stop slavery in places that
already had it. Southerners did not trust Lincoln or the
Republican Party. They linked him to the anti-slavery
movement because the Northern states had elected him.

Secession from the Union

Some Southern states declared their independence from the United
States because of their disagreements with the federal government.
Seceding states no longer followed the federal government's laws.
They no longer expected to get money, supplies, or services from
the federal government.

President Abraham
Lincoln took office
on March 4, 1861.
He would be
president during
one of the most
difficult times in
U.S. history.

South Carolina's Secession

In December 1860, South Carolina's leaders decided to secede and
become a **sovereign nation**. South Carolina would rule itself. Officials
in South Carolina waited to see what the federal government would do.
James Buchanan was president of the United States. Lincoln would not

> *This step, secession, once taken, can never be recalled. We and our posterity*
> *shall see our lovely South desolated by the demon of war.*
>
> —Alexander H. Stephens, the day before Georgia adopted the secession ordinance, January 18, 1861

take office until March 1861. Buchanan favored the South. He did not want to take action. He was willing to let South Carolina leave the Union.

Fort Sumter

Fort Sumter was a U.S. military base on an island in the harbor of Charleston, South Carolina. South Carolina wanted President Buchanan to remove the federal troops that were there. Buchanan had a problem. If he removed the troops, he would make his government angry. If he didn't, there would be more trouble with the Southern states. He decided that he would send supplies to Sumter, but he would not use a warship.

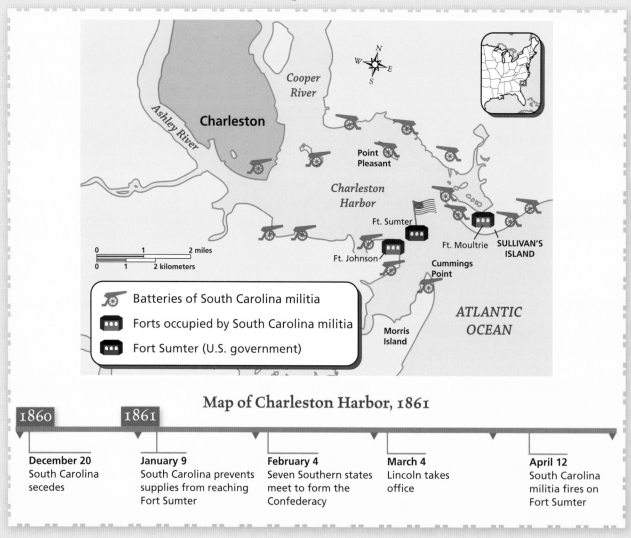

Map of Charleston Harbor, 1861

1860

December 20
South Carolina
secedes

1861

January 9
South Carolina prevents
supplies from reaching
Fort Sumter

February 4
Seven Southern states
meet to form the
Confederacy

March 4
Lincoln takes
office

April 12
South Carolina
militia fires on
Fort Sumter

On January 9, the **merchant ship** *Star of the West* arrived at Charleston Harbor, but it could not get to the fort. The South Carolina **militia** fired cannons at it. Major Robert Anderson was the commander of the federal troops at Fort Sumter. He had not received information that he was getting supplies. The ship turned around and the people of South Carolina celebrated. They saw this as a victory against the U.S. government.

The Confederate States of America

By the end of February 1861, Mississippi, Florida, Alabama, Georgia, Louisiana, and Texas joined South Carolina in seceding from the Union. These seven states decided to join together to form the Confederate States of America. They wrote their own constitution. They also elected their own president, Jefferson Davis. Davis had been a Mississippi senator and Secretary of War under President Franklin Pierce. He owned a plantation in Mississippi with many slaves.

Jefferson Davis was elected president of the Confederate States of America.

The Start of a New Nation

Since the new Confederate States of America did not have much money, it turned to Europe for help. The South knew that England and France needed its cotton. Also, a weaker, divided America was less of a threat to both countries. It could benefit England and France to support the Confederacy. However, England and France decided to wait.

The Confederacy began to take control of federal property within its borders. Fort Sumter was still under control of the United States. That upset the Confederates. It made it seem as though their new government did not have any power.

The Path to War

Seven Southern states had formed an independent nation, but most Southerners did not want war. Many people in both the North and South had mixed feelings about slavery and secession. They did not always agree with the actions of their governments. Also, neither side wanted to be the one that attacked first.

Lincoln's Inaugural Address

Lincoln became president on March 4, 1861. In his **inaugural address**, he sent a message to both Northern and Southern states. He said that secession was against the law. Therefore, the seceded states were still part of the Union. He also promised that he would not send federal troops against the Southern states or force them to end slavery. On the other hand, the U.S. government would also not give up any federal property in those states.

It was clear that Lincoln's words about federal property referred mainly to Fort Sumter. Confederates saw this as a declaration of war. No one, though, was ready to take the first step. Both sides waited to see what the other would do.

Crisis at Fort Sumter

After his inaugural address, President Lincoln learned that the commander of Fort Sumter, Major Anderson, was in serious trouble. His supplies and food were running out. Charleston Harbor was ringed with cannons aimed at Fort Sumter. There was no way to resupply the fort without starting a battle.

Lincoln had to make a decision. He had said in his inaugural address that he would not give up federal property. So if he gave up the fort, he would break that promise and seem weak. However, if he tried to resupply Sumter, it could be seen as an act of war.

Finally, after much thought, President Lincoln decided he would send supplies to Fort Sumter. He also sent a message to the governor of South Carolina. He told the governor that he was only sending **provisions**, not men, arms, or ammunition. The Confederates would have to make the decision to start a war.

> *So long as the United States keeps possession of this fort [Fort Sumter], the independence of South Carolina will only be in name, not in fact. If, however, it should be surrendered to South Carolina, which I do not apprehend, the smothered indignation of the free states would be roused beyond control.*
>
> —General John Wool, letter from Troy, New York, to a friend in Washington, DC, December 31, 1860

People in the War

Major Robert Anderson

Major Robert Anderson was the U.S. commander of Fort Sumter. Anderson was sympathetic to the South. He was from Kentucky and once owned slaves. However, he loved his country and did not think that the South should divide the Union.

Major Anderson was forced to surrender Fort Sumter in April 1861. After Charleston was recaptured by the Union four years later, he once again raised the U.S. flag over the fort.

The shelling of Fort Sumter by the South Carolina militia signaled the beginning of the Civil War.

The Attack on Fort Sumter

On April 9, Jefferson Davis and his **cabinet** met in Montgomery, Alabama, to discuss the situation at Fort Sumter. Davis ordered that the fort be fired on before the federal ships arrived with supplies. The attack on Fort Sumter began.

The Battle

Guns started firing on Fort Sumter on April 12, 1861, at 4:30 A.M. and continued for about 33 hours. Confederate forces shot about 4,000 shells at the fort, starting many fires and destroying parts of the fort. None of the men in the fort were killed, but they were worn out from fighting.

The guns at Fort Sumter returned fire at the South Carolina militia.

Major Anderson surrendered Fort Sumter on April 14. On that day, the Confederates took down the U.S. flag and raised the South Carolina militia flag over the fort.

The Effect on the North

The attack on Fort Sumter drove the North and South further apart. People in the North were angry. Even people who had been pro-South or undecided now wanted to defend the Union. President Lincoln planned to put down the rebellion. He asked the states for 75,000 volunteers.

The Effect on the South

Lincoln's call for troops forced people to take sides. None of the slave states still in the Union provided volunteers. Rather than send men to join Lincoln's army, more states left the Union. Virginia, North Carolina, Tennessee, and Arkansas seceded. Delaware, Maryland, Missouri, and Kentucky also threatened to leave. A new Confederate army began to form and the war had begun.

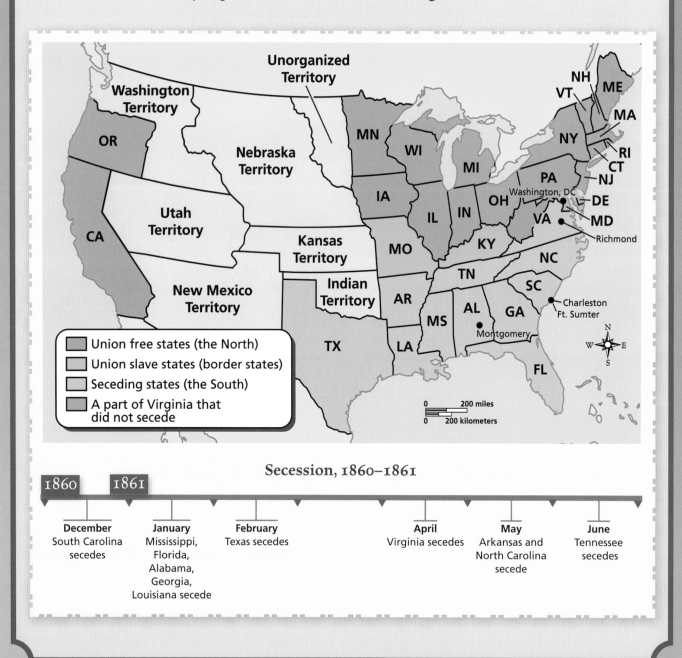

Secession, 1860–1861

1860	1861					
December South Carolina secedes	**January** Mississippi, Florida, Alabama, Georgia, Louisiana secede	**February** Texas secedes		**April** Virginia secedes	**May** Arkansas and North Carolina secede	**June** Tennessee secedes

Map legend:
- Union free states (the North)
- Union slave states (border states)
- Seceding states (the South)
- A part of Virginia that did not secede

2 The First Battles

T he surrender of Fort Sumter showed that the South had the power to fight. Now both sides could see that there was little chance of avoiding a war.

Fighting for American Values

Those in the Union and those in the Confederacy felt they were defending the values that Americans fought for in the Revolutionary War. Northerners thought that American democracy was the best in the world. They wanted to keep the states together because their ancestors had died to create the United States of America. They wanted to fight for their country and the **rights** that were in the **U.S. Constitution**.

Southerners felt that the North had changed what the Constitution stood for. They believed that American democracy meant that people should have the right to decide how to live. If the people of a state wanted to own slaves or did not want to be a part of the Union anymore, they had the right to decide this for themselves.

Many people were very excited about a war. They didn't think it would last long—maybe three months at the most. The first Union **volunteers** were asked to sign up for only 90 days. Young men rushed to join up for the adventure and glory of battle. They were worried that the war would end before they had a chance to fight. Soon enough it became clear that the war would last longer than anyone expected.

Major Events

1861

April 14
Fort Sumter surrenders to the Confederates

April 17
Virginia secedes

May 23
Alexandria, Virginia, is captured by Union troops

July 21
The First Battle of Manassas

The Confederacy Grows

The states of Arkansas, Tennessee, North Carolina, and Virginia were on the border between the North and the South. When Abraham Lincoln called on citizens to join the army, these states had to decide whether to stay in the Union or join the Southern states and secede. Slavery was allowed in these states, although most people did not own slaves. There were economic, political, and social ties to both the North and the South. After debating what to do, these states decided they would join the Confederacy. They seceded in April and May of 1861.

The Importance of Virginia

Without these Upper South states, the Confederacy did not have much chance of winning the war. The original seven Deep South states had a much smaller population than the North and very little industry.

Virginia had a large population that was willing to fight. Some of the South's most brilliant leaders came from that state. Virginia was both an agricultural and industrial leader in the South. Wealthy, **prominent** men owned large plantations with many slaves. Many of the factories of Southern industry were located in Virginia. Most important, it was close to important railroad and water transportation routes. It was also right next to Washington, DC, the capital of the United States.

West Virginia is Formed

Even in Virginia, though, there was debate about joining the Confederacy. Eastern Virginia was home to wealthy plantation owners who owned slaves and supported secession. Many of the farmers in western Virginia wanted to remain in the Union. After Virginia seceded in April, western farmers met in June and voted to secede from Virginia and return to the Union.

> "
> *A warning to secessionist traitors in our midst. Western Virginia will Secede from eastern Virginia, if she Secedes from the Union.*
>
> —Wheeling Daily Intelligencer
> "

The Border States Decide

Maryland, Delaware, Missouri, and Kentucky were also on the border. They had to decide which side to join. Slavery was allowed in these states, but many people believed that it would eventually be abolished. People in these states were divided. Members of the same family often held different opinions.

At first, these states tried not to take sides and to remain **neutral**. However, there were fights and even violent battles between Union supporters and Confederate secessionists.

The Importance of Maryland

The location of the border states made them important to both the Union and the Confederacy. Kentucky and Missouri had rivers that flowed south. Control of these rivers would allow armies to either threaten or protect the South.

Maryland was also in a strategic position, between Washington, DC, and the North, and adjacent to Virginia. Northern troops had to pass through Maryland to get to the capital. Maryland's waterways and railroads were used to move men and supplies.

The Tension Builds

Many people in Maryland wanted to join the Confederacy. They did not want Union soldiers in their state. On April 19, 1861, a riot started in Baltimore when troops from Massachusetts were attacked on their way to protect Washington, DC. Some telegraph lines and railroad bridges leading to Washington were destroyed.

Despite the violence, Maryland did not join the Confederacy. It became more pro-Union as more Northern soldiers poured into the state. Still, many citizens continued to help the Confederate cause.

On April 25, 1861, troops from throughout the Union arrived in Washington, D.C. Soldiers slept in the House of Congress and the **rotunda** of the Capitol. Soon there were camps of Union soldiers all around the city.

To protect Washington, Lincoln sent troops into Virginia, to the nearby towns of Arlington and Alexandria. Both were quickly captured. In Alexandria, a popular Union officer, Colonel Elmer

What Do You Know!

Kentucky and Missouri were so deeply divided that they had two governments—one supporting the Confederacy and one supporting the Union. In 1863, Missouri supplied 39 regiments for the siege of Vicksburg—22 for the Union and 17 for the Confederacy.

Ellsworth, tore down a Confederate flag from a hotel. He was killed by the hotelkeeper. Many Northerners wanted revenge for Ellsworth's death.

Building an Army

When the South seceded, it had to start its own War Department and army. The North already had troops and a navy. However, neither side was prepared to fight a large war. Armies and navies require many different types of supplies, and plenty of them.

Departments within the War Department for each side set about manufacturing or buying many things. The Ordnance Department was responsible for the many types of weapons, from muskets and rifles to cannons and mortars, as well as materials to repair them and ammunition.

The Commissary Department was responsible for food. The Quartermaster Department was responsible for everything else: uniforms, tents, wagons and other transportation, horses, and even paper.

Once supplies were obtained, the departments needed to figure out how to get them to the troops. Keeping troops supplied often affected military **strategy**. Troops who marched too far from a supply line risked being cut off.

Troops and supplies were transported to the front by railroad.

The North's Advantage

At the start of the war, the Union had a huge need for supplies for the first 75,000 volunteers. Most of the army's weapons, ammunition, cloth, iron, and shoes were made in northern factories. The North also had many railroads and water routes for moving supplies. It had many good roads. Northern industry was quick to turn its efforts to supplying the army.

The Confederacy had many problems to overcome. Its population was smaller than the North. There were also fewer resources. The South grew enough food to supply its troops, but there were few ways to transport the food. There were also not as many factories to make the supplies the army needed.

Support for the South

The Confederacy turned to Europe for help. British textile mills depended on cotton grown in the South to make cloth. The British government wanted to help the South because it could make money selling supplies to the Confederacy. Britain also wanted to ensure that it would continue to get cotton for its factories.

However, the people of England were against slavery. England had banned the slave trade in 1807 and abolished slavery in 1833. The English government did not want to anger its citizens. Although it helped the South, it would not support it openly. The South had to prove that it was strong enough to survive. Then it might get more help from Europe.

The First Armies

Both sides had to turn volunteers away because they did not have enough equipment. Soldiers often brought their own weapons and horses and even silverware. Some Southerners brought their slaves to serve them in camp, cook their food, and take care of their horses. Both the Union and Confederate armies enlisted white men only, although many African-American men tried to join the Union army. African-American drill companies were organized in cities across the North, but it was not until 1863 that African Americans were allowed to enlist in the U.S. Army.

ORGANIZATION Many of the men on both sides were part of volunteer militias in their towns. A militia was a small unit that could be called upon by a state in times of need. Militias usually were not well trained. They combined with other militias to form state regiments. **Regiments** consisted of about 1,000 men each. The regiments then formed larger units, such as divisions. **Divisions** could have 12,000 men. The men from these units joined thousands of other men to march into battle.

PREPARATION Training usually began when soldiers joined a division. However, there often wasn't enough time to give the men all the training they needed. Many men went into battle unprepared.

At first, the Union and the Confederacy could not even supply their troops with proper uniforms. In early battles, each regiment wore its own colors. This caused mixups on the battlefield. It was hard to tell which side people were fighting on. Eventually Northern soldiers wore blue uniforms and Southern troops wore gray.

Going to Battle

Both sides prepared for war but had different **strategies**. The North made plans to attack. However, President Lincoln and other Northern leaders did not want to take over the South. They wanted to end the war quickly and avoid too much bloodshed.

The South's strategy was to wait for the North to invade. The longer it waited, the more time it had to prepare its troops. The South would defend important areas and simply try not to lose.

The Anaconda Plan

General Winfield Scott was commander of the Union army at the beginning of the Civil War.

The commander of the U.S. Army was General Winfield Scott. He had a plan to cut off the secessionists. He thought this would convince pro-Union Southerners to turn against their leaders.

The first part of Scott's plan was to capture Richmond, Virginia. Richmond was the Confederate capital. It was about 100 miles (161 km) from Washington, DC. Scott also planned to send the U.S. Navy to **blockade** the seacoast of the Southern states. This would prevent Southern states from trading with other countries. Then Scott planned to move troops down the Mississippi River to cut the South in half. That would divide the South's armies and make them easier to defeat.

Scott knew his strategy would take a lot of time. He wanted to build up the navy. He also thought the new soldiers needed more time to train.

Newspapers made fun of the idea and called it the Anaconda Plan. They said it was like an anaconda—a snake that squeezes its prey. Scott wanted "to squeeze the South to military death." But Northerners did not want to wait. They wanted to crush the rebels right away.

> *If I could only get the enemy to attack me, as I am trying to have him do, I would stake my reputation on the handsomest victory that could be hoped for.*
>
> —Confederate General P.G.T. Beauregard, letter to Congressman L. T. Wigfall, July 8, 1861

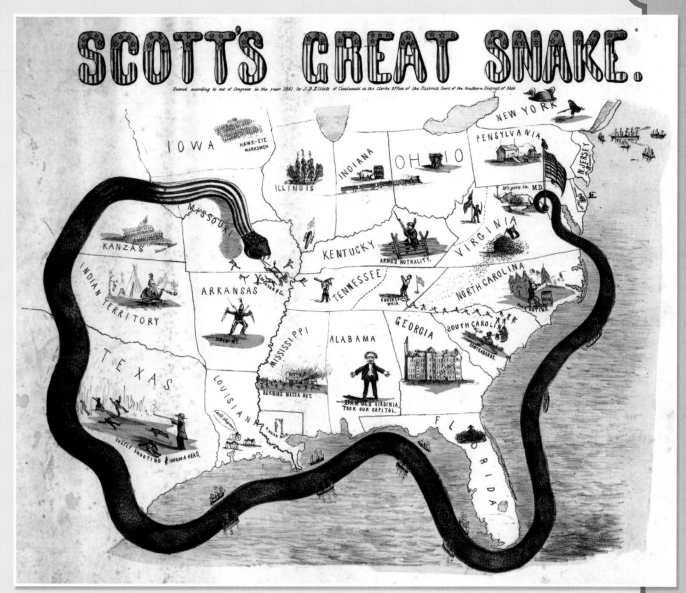

The First Battles

Union troops were sent to the western part of Virginia. This area sided more with the Union. It also had important railroad connections to other states. The commander of the Union troops was General George McClellan. Union and Confederate troops met at Fairfax Courthouse, Philippi, and Corrick's Ford. McClellan's victories over the outnumbered Confederate forces increased public confidence in the final outcome. Northerners began to believe that all they had to do was march to Richmond and throw the Confederate government out.

This cartoon from 1861 pokes fun at General Winfield Scott's plan to blockade and split the Confederacy.

On to Richmond!

Northern newspapers and leaders started the call to move on to Richmond. The Confederate Congress planned to meet there on July 20. Northerners wanted the city to be in Union hands by then.

Manassas

The way to Richmond was blocked by almost 22,000 Confederate troops in Manassas, Virginia. Manassas was a small town only about 30 miles (48 km) from Washington, DC. It had an important railroad line that connected the Northeast to the South. It was also close enough to launch an attack on the U.S. capital.

President Lincoln felt pressured to make the next move. He thought that capturing Richmond would be a big blow against the secessionists.

Preparing for Battle

General Irvin McDowell was put in command of the U.S. troops. The commander of the Confederate troops was General P.G.T. Beauregard. Neither commander had much experience in battle and the largely volunteer troops were not well trained.

THE NORTH'S PLAN McDowell had over 35,000 men. His army was larger than the Confederate forces. However, another 12,000 Confederate soldiers were in the Shenandoah Valley under the command of General Joseph Johnston. Johnston's men could reach Manassas in just a few days. If he joined with Beauregard, McDowell would be outnumbered.

A Union army was also in the Shenandoah Valley. It was commanded by General Robert Patterson. McDowell was counting on Patterson to keep Johnston's soldiers from leaving the Shenandoah Valley.

THE SOUTH'S RESPONSE On July 16, McDowell's army began its march from Washington to Manassas. Beauregard knew that his Confederate troops were outnumbered. He needed Johnston's extra forces.

As soon as McDowell left Washington, Beauregard ordered Johnston to move his troops by railroad to Manassas. To do this, Johnston had to keep Patterson from guessing his plans. Johnston tricked Patterson into thinking that the Confederates were about to attack. Patterson thought he was outnumbered. While he backed off, Johnston was able to slip away.

🌠 What Do You Know!

NAMING THE BATTLES
The North and South had different ways to name battles. The South usually named a battle after the town where it was fought. The South named this battle Manassas, after the railroad terminal.

The North usually named battles after landmarks. Often it was a river or stream. In this case, Bull Run was the name of the stream where this battle took place.

The First Battle of Manassas

General McDowell's march to Manassas should only have taken a few days. His soldiers, though, were barely trained. They were not used to walking long distances or waiting for orders. The march was very slow. Men would walk off to find water or lie down to rest when they were tired. McDowell had to stop to wait for supplies and organize the troops. He was finally ready to attack on the morning of July 21.

Manassas was so close to Washington that hundreds of reporters, congressmen, and other civilians came to watch the battle. They sat on a hill two miles (3 km) from the battle. Many brought picnic baskets and wine. It was like watching a sports match.

A Union brigade attacks the Confederates at the First Battle of Manassas.

The Attack

General Beauregard decided the Confederate forces would fight by a stream called Bull Run. This battle would come to be called the Battle of Manassas in the South and the Battle of Bull Run in the North. At first, Union forces overwhelmed the Confederates. Southern troops retreated to a hill called Henry House Hill.

By then, most of Johnston's troops had arrived by train. Since they did not have to march, the men were still fresh. The Union soldiers were exhausted, thirsty, and hungry. Many had simply left the battlefield. They were overwhelmed by the new Confederate **reinforcements**.

The Confederates advanced and grew stronger. The Northerners couldn't hold them off. They retreated in a panic. Even the people picnicking on the hill ran off in fright. Confederate soldiers followed, but they were too tired and disorganized to go far.

> *Today will be known as BLACK MONDAY. We are utterly and disgracefully routed, beaten, whipped by secessionists.*
>
> —George Templeton Strong, of New York City, diary entry upon hearing of the Union loss at the First Battle of Bull Run, July 21, 1861

People in the War

Stonewall Jackson

One of the bravest Confederate leaders at Manassas was Thomas Jackson. He became one of the most important generals in the war.

Jackson had trained his troops well. They stood strong against Union forces. To encourage his own troops, a Southern general yelled: "There stands Jackson like a stone wall!" The nickname "Stonewall" stuck to Jackson from then on.

The Results

The battle went on for one day, and about 4,500 men were killed, wounded, or missing. Some men ran away. Others were taken prisoner.

The soldiers who fought that day were unprepared. Men did not follow orders. Often there was complete confusion. Many Confederate soldiers still did not wear the gray uniforms of the South. It was hard to tell who was a friend and who was an enemy.

Victory for the South

The South was overjoyed with its victory. It gave its army more confidence. The South began to believe it could win. In the North, leaders were less sure that they could easily defeat the Confederates. However, the battle made Northerners even more eager to continue the fight.

Both sides called for hundreds of thousands of volunteers. But soldiers were now expected to serve for three years. People could see that it would be a long war. It was not a sporting event. One side was not going to defeat the other in one glorious battle.

Stonewall Jackson with his men at the First Battle of Manassas.

Western Theater Battles

The defeat at Manassas gave the South reason to believe it could win the war. President Lincoln worried that the loss would lead to trouble in the border states of Kentucky, Missouri, and Maryland. Those states had remained neutral and not taken sides.

Importance of the Border States

The Confederate victory at Manassas encouraged those who supported secession in the border states. If one of those states decided to secede, the other two might follow. All three states were in very important locations. Maryland was right next to Washington, DC, and Kentucky and Missouri were gateways to the West.

Kentucky and Missouri had men and supplies that both armies needed. These states also had important rivers running through them: the Mississippi, the Missouri, the Ohio, the Tennessee, and the Cumberland. These rivers were important routes through Northern and Southern states. Boats could easily move supplies and troops.

Major Events

1861

July 21
First Battle of Manassas

September 4
The Confederate army invades Kentucky

1862

February 6
Battle of Fort Henry

February 11–16
Battle of Fort Donelson

April 6–7
Battle of Shiloh

> *I hold that, in contemplation of universal law, and of the Constitution, the Union of these states is perpetual.*
>
> —Abraham Lincoln, March 4, 1861

The Strategy in the West

The Union felt pressure to fight harder after its loss at Manassas. Leaders were afraid that the defeat made them look weak and would encourage more people to side with the Confederacy.

The Union's strategy was to divide Confederate forces by attacking in the East and the West. The Confederate army had to defend a huge area. It didn't have enough men to protect every important position.

Keeping Kentucky Neutral

Kentucky bordered three free states and three slave states. Kentucky was a slave state. It had strong economic and social ties to both the North and the South, so Kentucky officially remained neutral on secession.

> *I hope to have God on my side, but I must have Kentucky.*
> —attributed to Abraham Lincoln

It's citizens, however, were fiercely divided. The governor was secessionist, but the **legislature** was Unionist. This division was seen even within families. First Lady Mary Todd Lincoln's sisters, for example, were married to Confederate generals. Both the United States and Confederate governments did not want to upset Kentucky's neutral position. They did not want to do anything that would cause Kentucky to choose the other side, but both sides wanted the natural and human resources Kentucky held. While Kentucky did not send troops to either the Union or Confederate armies, recruiters were busy throughout the state.

The Balance Is Disrupted

The Union built a large military and naval base in Cairo, Illinois, where the Ohio River joins the Mississippi River. Cairo is in the southern tip of Illinois and lies between Missouri and Kentucky. The Union hoped that a show of force there would convince Confederate forces not to invade Kentucky.

A large number of Confederate troops were stationed nearby in Tennessee. On September 4, 1861, General Leonidas Polk ordered Confederate troops into Kentucky. They captured the city of Columbus, which was an important railroad center. They built a fort on the bluffs overlooking the river to prevent Union troops from venturing into Kentucky.

Kentuckians were alarmed by this violation of their neutrality. The legislature became even more in favor of the Union and wanted the Confederates out of their state. The legislature invited Union troops into the state to help them.

The First Battles for Kentucky

General Albert Sidney Johnston commanded Confederate troops in the West. Johnston faced Union troops commanded by General Ulysses S. Grant. Grant moved from Cairo to Paducah, Kentucky. He prepared to attack two Confederate bases: Fort Henry and Fort Donelson.

Confederate Defenses

The Confederates thought Union forces would first attack along the Mississippi, so they strengthened forts there. Fort Henry was positioned to control traffic on the Tennessee River. Fort Donelson guarded the Cumberland River. Grant thought they were weak points in the South's defense. These rivers could be a highway into the Deep South for Union troops. Once these forts were gone, it would be easier to capture other important targets.

Fort Henry

On February 6, 1862, Union Naval officer Andrew Foote opened fire on Fort Henry from new ironclad gunboats. The plan was for the boats to attack the fort while Grant's troops surrounded it. The bombardment was too much for the poorly built fort and it fell even before Grant arrived. The Confederates realized they were in danger. The commander took most of his men to nearby Fort Donelson before Fort Henry surrendered. With the capture of Fort Henry, the North now had a water route to important Confederate centers.

Fort Donelson

Fort Donelson was about 11 miles (18 km) from Fort Henry. Fort Donelson was more of a challenge to Grant and Foote. It was better constructed than Fort Henry. It was located on high ground and

Albert Sidney Johnston was commander of Confederate troops in the West. He was killed in April 1862 at the Battle of Shiloh.

Kansas

Missouri

IL

IN

Louisville

Kentucky

Virginia

Perryville

Ft. Donelson

Paducah

Ohio R.

North Carolina

Ft. Henry

Nashville

Arkansas R.

Memphis

Tennessee

Chattanooga

Indian Territory

Pea Ridge (Elkhorn Tavern)

Shiloh (Pittsburg Landing)

South Carolina

Arkansas

Mississippi R.

Corinth

ATLANTIC OCEAN

Birmingham

Atlanta

Red River

Dallas

Mississippi

Alabama

Georgia

Louisiana

Jackson

Montgomery

Texas

Mobile

Florida

Houston

Baton Rouge

New Orleans

Gulf of Mexico

	Union states
	Confederate states of America
	Union victory

0   125   250 miles
0   125   250 kilometers

Battle of Pea Ridge
March 7-8

Battles in the West, 1861-1862

1862

February 6
Battle of Ft. Henry

February 11–16
Battle of Ft. Donelson

April 6–7
Battle of Shiloh

October 3–4
Battle of Corinth

October 8
Battle of Perryville

protected from both land and water attacks. Grant arrived on February 12 with 15,000 men and began to surround the fort. Occasional clashes broke out, but the fort held Grant off.

Two days later, Grant welcomed another 10,000 men and Foote and his gunboats arrived. Foote's boats, however, were too close. Their shells went over the fort. The guns in the fort were able to hit the boats, though. Two were sunk and four were damaged, forcing Foote to retreat.

FORT DONELSON SURRENDERS Since the fort could not be taken by water, Grant attacked by land. With more gunfire from the boats, Grant was finally able to defeat the Confederates. Thousands of men were killed or wounded. Many froze in the terrible cold. The two top commanders of the fort escaped in boats during the night. Another officer refused to surrender and led 700 men through icy streams to Nashville, Tennessee.

An officer named Simon Buckner was left in command of Fort Donelson. Grant demanded **unconditional surrender**. Buckner had no choice but to give up everything. He turned over about 13,000 men, 65 cannons, 20,000 rifles, and 4,000 horses. These were big losses for the Confederate army.

THE RESULTS News of the victories at Fort Henry and Fort Donelson sent cheers throughout the North. The Union now controlled important rivers and railroads. Lincoln made Grant second-in-command in the West.

The Confederates were in despair. The South had lost about one third of its troops based in the Western theater. In February 1862, Nashville, Tennessee, also fell to the North. It was the first Confederate state capital to be captured.

Kentucky and most of Tennessee were now in Union hands. From there, Union troops could march further into the South. The Confederate army was in a difficult position. Its commanders had to rethink their strategy.

The Battle of Shiloh

Confederate General Albert Sidney Johnston moved his troops to Corinth, Mississippi. The town was near the Tennessee border. There he gathered a force of 40,000 soldiers. He and General Beauregard decided to march north and retake Tennessee.

Pittsburgh Landing

Grant was sent to Pittsburgh Landing on the Tennessee River, about 23 miles (37 km) from Corinth. There he was to meet up with General Don Carlos Buell's Army of the Ohio. Buell was coming from Nashville, about 135 miles (217 km) away.

Grant had around 40,000 soldiers in his Army of the Tennessee. With Buell's men they would have a total force of about 65,000. Grant's

People in the War

General Ulysses S. Grant

Ulysses S. Grant was not always a respected commander. He had graduated at the bottom of his class from West Point. He had left the army once because of a charge of drunkenness. When war broke out, he volunteered for duty and was accepted because the army needed officers.

Grant's initiative and success in Kentucky proved that he was a great fighting leader, and he earned Lincoln's respect. Soon Lincoln made him the commander of all the Union forces.

troops waited almost a month for Buell's men. He spent the time drilling his men, since many were new recruits. Grant did not have his men **fortify** their position. This was to be a fatal mistake.

Johnston and Beauregard decided to attack Pittsburgh Landing before Buell arrived. On April 3, 1862, Johnston began marching north. Heavy rains and untested soldiers slowed his advance. The Confederate forces finally arrived on April 5.

Day One

Johnston stopped a few miles (km) from the Union campsite. He spent a day organizing his troops. Even though his men made noise and lit campfires, the Union army was unaware of their presence. Grant and his commanders did not expect to be attacked. They were not ready to defend themselves.

THE ATTACK On the morning of April 6, Johnston attacked. There were thick woods and rugged terrain. Some men got lost. It was difficult to give orders, but Johnston and his men still surprised the Union troops.

Thousands of Confederate soldiers came spilling out of the woods near Shiloh Church. Some Union officers in the camps understood what was happening and tried to prepare their men, but it was not enough. Soon the untrained men of both sides were out of control.

Union soldiers fled. Confederate soldiers stopped to steal things from the tents in the camp. Many of the soldiers were starving. They ate the breakfasts that the Northerners had left behind.

THE BATTLE Eight out of ten men fighting that day had never been in a battle before. Many from both sides hid or fled in terror. There was confusion and panic everywhere.

> ❝
> *I would fight them if they were a million. They can present no greater front between those two creeks than we can, and the more men they crowd in there, the worse we can make it for them.*
>
> —Confederate General Albert Sidney Johnston, to his officers, at Shiloh, TN, April 6, 1862
> ❞

🌠 What Do You Know!

SHILOH CHURCH

The battle that took place in Pittsburgh Landing was named after a small church where the attack started. The name *Shiloh* is from a Hebrew word meaning "place of peace."

General Grant was across the river waiting for Buell to arrive. When he heard gunfire, he took a boat up the river to Pittsburgh Landing. He reached the battle by around 9:00 A.M. By then, the fighting was at full force. Confederate troops pushed back the Union forces. Grant and his commanders tried to bring the scattered men under control.

Johnston saw his chance. He led a charge that inspired his tired Confederate troops. During the fighting, he was wounded in his leg. He didn't realize how much he was bleeding. Johnston kept fighting, but he finally collapsed and died. General Beauregard quickly took over the command.

The Southern forces were winning, but one group of Union soldiers held out. About 11,000 men had retreated to a wooded area that was later named the Hornets' Nest for the heavy swarm of their bullets. For six hours they fought off the Confederates. The 2,200 survivors finally surrendered just before nightfall, but they had bought valuable time for Union troops. Beauregard called off the attack for the night. He sent a message to Jefferson Davis that the South had won.

> *The gory corpses lying all around us, in every imaginable attitude, and slain by an inconceivable variety of wound, were shocking to behold.*
>
> —Union soldier, recalling the first day's battle at Shiloh, April 5, 1862

The Union army's victory at the Battle of Shiloh (Pittsburgh Landing) enabled it to capture much of Tennessee.

Day Two

General Beauregard had guessed wrong. The battle at the Hornets' Nest had given Grant valuable time. He began to build a defense near Pittsburgh Landing, where two gunboats were docked.

Also during the night, Buell's troops finally began to arrive. Boats carried them across the river. By morning, 25,000 fresh reinforcements had joined Grant's tired army. Some Confederates saw Buell's men coming off the boats. However, Beauregard could not be found and no one seemed to be in charge.

The next day, Grant and his men went on the attack. The worn-out Southern troops could not hold them back. The rebel army lost all the ground it had taken the day before. At around 3:00 P.M., Beauregard ordered his soldiers to retreat.

The Results of the Battle

Shiloh was the bloodiest battle of the war to that point. Almost 24,000 men were either killed or wounded in two days. That was one out of every four men who fought. The bodies were buried in **mass graves**.

The Union Gains Control

After Shiloh, the U.S. Army combined its troops to form a huge force of about 120,000 men. They marched slowly toward Corinth to capture the railroad center there. General Beauregard knew that his Confederate force had no chance against such a large army. He pulled his men out of Corinth and retreated further into Mississippi.

By June, the South had lost Kentucky and most of Tennessee. It had also lost control of three important waterways, including the Mississippi River. Shiloh was a terrible defeat for the Confederacy and a turning point in the war.

The Effect on the Nation

The bloody results at Shiloh shocked people in the North and the South. They now realized that neither side would give up easily. General Grant understood the change that had come about. After Shiloh, he said later, he "gave up all idea of saving the Union except by complete conquest."

Eastern Theater Battles

The Battle of Manassas had been an embarrassing defeat for the North. Lincoln needed a victory. When General Winfield Scott retired, Lincoln had to find a new general-in-chief. In November 1861, Lincoln chose General George B. McClellan.

The New General

General McClellan had led successful battles in western Virginia. Those victories helped West Virginia break away from the rest of Virginia and rejoin the Union when Virginia seceded. McClellan was also very good at organizing and training troops. His men loved him. They called him "Little Mac."

Confederate troops still held the area around Manassas. Union troops in the East had done nothing since they lost that part of Virginia. Lincoln wanted McClellan to come up with a plan that would win the war soon. The president thought it was important to capture Richmond, the Confederate capital. McClellan wanted time to prepare. He decided to move his large army in the spring.

> **"** He who does something at the head of one Regiment, will eclipse him who does nothing at the head of a hundred.
>
> —Abraham Lincoln **"**

Major Events
1862

March 11
McClellan starts his Peninsula Campaign

March–June
"Stonewall" Jackson's Shenandoah Valley Campaign

May 24
McClellan reaches Richmond, Virginia

May 31
Seven Pines Battle

June 25–July 1
Seven Days Battles

McClellan's Peninsula Campaign

McClellan's plan was different from President Lincoln's. Lincoln wanted his general to take Manassas and then move on to Richmond. He was unhappy that McClellan was taking so long to act.

McClellan's army outnumbered Confederate forces. However, he worried that it would be difficult to march through Confederate defenses in northern Virginia. McClellan planned to go around Manassas and come up from the south. He would move troops and supplies by boat to Fort Monroe at the tip of the York-James peninsula. From there, he could march straight up to Richmond.

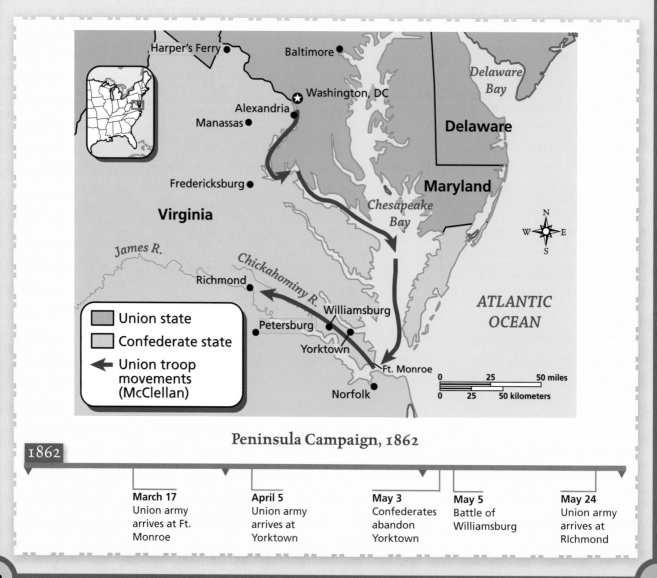

Peninsula Campaign, 1862

1862

March 17
Union army arrives at Ft. Monroe

April 5
Union army arrives at Yorktown

May 3
Confederates abandon Yorktown

May 5
Battle of Williamsburg

May 24
Union army arrives at RIchmond

Lincoln agreed to McClellan's plan. He ordered some troops to stay behind to protect Washington. He also relieved McClellan of the position of general-in-chief so he could focus on taking Richmond. At last, McClellan began his **campaign,** seven months after he took command.

Yorktown

McClellan arrived at Fort Monroe on March 17, 1862. Boats delivered 121,500 men, 14,500 horses and mules, hundreds of cannons, tons of food and supplies, and even telegraph wire and bridges. The large army started its march north, but muddy roads and incorrect maps slowed it down. McClellan's force arrived in Yorktown on April 5. The Confederates were already there.

The Confederate commander was General Joseph E. Johnston. McClellan had taken so long to start his campaign that Johnston had plenty of time to send troops to the peninsula to meet him. In Yorktown, there were only about 17,000 Confederates to fight McClellan. By constant movement, they fooled McClellan into thinking he faced a much larger force.

General George McClellan led Union forces in the Peninsula Campaign.

McClellan decided to spend a month digging **trenches** and placing guns. Reinforcements joined the Confederate troops and there were small **skirmishes**. Finally, on May 3, McClellan felt ready to blast the Confederates with the huge guns he had put in place. Before he could start, the Confederates disappeared. Knowing they couldn't win, they had left Yorktown overnight.

Threat to Richmond

From Yorktown, McClellan moved to Williamsburg. There, his troops had their first real battle on May 5. There were almost 4,000 **casualties**, but the Southern troops were forced to retreat, leaving eastern Virginia in Union control.

The two armies continued up the peninsula toward Richmond. Traveling conditions were terrible for the soldiers and there was constant rain and mud. Many men got sick. By May 24, Union troops were about six miles (10 km) from Richmond. Many people in Richmond panicked and fled the city.

Although he held the advantage, McClellan would not attack. Once again he thought he was outnumbered. He waited for Lincoln to send reinforcements. Lincoln was angry that his general would not move, but he agreed to send more men. McClellan waited. This gave Confederate leaders time to plan their own attack. It was vital for them to win this battle.

Action in the Shenandoah Valley

General McClellan's delays caused many problems. Union leaders were angry that he did not act because they believed he could win. Some thought he was **betraying** his country. McClellan had also taken many troops away from the capital. The government was afraid that there were not enough soldiers to protect Washington, DC.

McClellan's lack of action helped the South. They were weak compared to the North because they did not have as many men and supplies. McClellan's reluctance gave the Confederate forces time to move to critical areas. They had time to decide on different strategies to defeat the North.

One area that benefited from the Confederates' ability to plan was the Shenandoah Valley, in western Virginia. This area was a **breadbasket** of the Confederacy, that provided a great deal of food for the Confederate armies. Roads and railroads for moving troops and supplies were located there. The South desperately needed to keep this region. The man they put in charge was Stonewall Jackson. Jackson complicated the war for the North.

Jackson Surprises the North

Stonewall Jackson demanded a lot from his men, and they respected him. His troops often won in battle because they were well trained.

Confederate leaders wanted Jackson to keep Union forces busy in the Shenandoah Valley. If Union soldiers were fighting Jackson, they couldn't help McClellan on the peninsula. This strategy worked. Even with only 4,200 men, Jackson caused a lot of trouble.

KERNSTOWN On March 23, Jackson attacked a much larger Union force. He lost the battle. However, his actions still helped Southern efforts.

> *Give me ten thousand men, and I would be in Washington tomorrow.*
>
> —Stonewall Jackson

Lincoln thought Jackson must have a large army to make such a bold attack. The president worried that there weren't enough troops to defend the Shenandoah Valley. He also worried that Jackson was close enough to attack Washington, DC.

Lincoln refused to send more troops to McClellan in Yorktown. Instead, he sent a larger force to the Shenandoah Valley. He also ordered a large army to stay near the capital. McClellan was angry about the reinforcements. He blamed Lincoln and other leaders for many of his problems.

CONFUSING THE ENEMY Union troops chased Jackson up and down the valley. Jackson continued to attack them. Jackson now had a force of 16,000 men, but they were still outnumbered by the Union forces they faced. Lincoln sent three generals and three armies to stop him, but they never could.

Jackson had another advantage as well. He had a detailed map of the area. He used the map to find unusual routes to surprise his enemies. It also helped him disappear if he needed to make a quick escape.

Stonewall Jackson led Confederate forces in the Shenandoah Valley campaign.

Jackson the Hero

By May, General McClellan was on the march to Richmond. The Confederate army needed more soldiers to fight him. They thought about bringing Jackson's troops to the peninsula. Instead, they decided he would do more good if he stayed in the valley.

Jackson's brave actions made Washington nervous. Lincoln ordered reinforcements for McClellan, then he changed his mind when Jackson gained another victory.

In about two months, Jackson's small army had fought off 64,000 Union troops and captured a large amount of supplies. They had marched almost 680 miles (1,094 km) in about 48 days. Union casualties numbered 7,000 compared to 2,500 Confederate casualties.

Jackson chased the Union troops out of the Shenandoah Valley. His victories came at a time when the South felt defeated. He inspired the Confederates to continue their fight.

The Fight for Richmond

Jackson was still in the Shenandoah Valley when Joseph Johnston made his first move to defend Richmond. General McClellan's troops were very close to the city. The Confederates knew that if they lost Richmond, the capital of the Confederacy, they could soon lose the war.

The Battle of Seven Pines

The Union forces were camped on both sides of the Chickahominy River. Heavy rains had caused the river to rise. On May 30, a storm destroyed the bridges the soldiers had built over the river. McClellan's army was divided in two. General Johnston decided to attack the side of the river where the Union army was weakest.

The battle was a disaster. At first, Confederate forces were able to drive Union troops back. By that evening, some Union soldiers were able to cross the river to fight. Confederate troops were disorganized and the chain of command broke down. By the next day, the Confederates had lost all the ground they had gained.

There were about 5,000 Union casualties and 6,000 Confederate casualties. Some areas were so flooded that wounded soldiers had to sit up so they wouldn't drown.

Joseph Johnston was badly wounded during the battle. Confederate President Jefferson Davis needed to replace his general. He chose Robert E. Lee as the new commander of the Confederate army.

The Seven Days Battles

General Lee took a month to prepare. He had his troops dig trenches around Richmond. He brought troops in from the lower South and even secretly sent for Stonewall Jackson.

McClellan and Lee's own men thought that he was digging trenches to defend Richmond against a Union attack. But Lee wanted to save Richmond by forcing the Union troops out of Virginia entirely.

McClellan discovered that Jackson was coming. Once again, he worried that he did not have enough men. McClellan's army consisted of about 115,000 soldiers. He thought the Confederate force had about 200,000 men. In fact, there were only about 90,000.

THE FIRST BATTLES On June 25, the two sides fought a large skirmish. It was the first of six battles that took place over seven days. The next day, McClellan was finally ready to attack Richmond, but Lee attacked first in Mechanicsville. His troops lost the fight.

McClellan called the battle a "complete victory" for the North. General Lee, though, had made some important gains. His actions stopped McClellan from attacking Richmond. The Union troops fell back to higher and safer ground. Instead of attacking, they waited for Lee to make the next move.

On June 27, Confederate troops defeated a smaller Union force in Gaines' Mill. It was a bloody battle with about 15,000 casualties. This convinced McClellan to give up on capturing Richmond. He decided to move to the James River, where there were U.S. warships.

THE BATTLE OF MALVERN HILL Over the next four days, the two armies fought three more battles. Lee continued to attack, even though his troops had many casualties.

In the sixth and final battle, McClellan held a strong position on Malvern Hill. He had 100 cannons in the front and 150 on the **flanks**. Lee used every available soldier he could. He wanted to trap McClellan's troops by the James River, but the Confederates had to attack by crossing a wide open plain. They were blasted by Union guns. Over 5,000 Confederate soldiers were lost. Union forces had 3,000 casualties.

> *It was not war. It was murder.*
> —Confederate Commander Daniel Harvey Hill, describing the Battle of Malvern Hill

These Confederate soldiers of the Third Georgia Infantry fought at Malvern Hill.

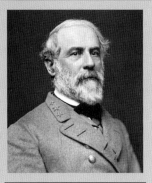

People in the War

Robert E. Lee

Robert E. Lee was a graduate of West Point. He had served in the United States Army in the Mexican War. Lee was initially offered a position in the Union army. When Virginia seceded, he chose to serve his state instead. Until Seven Pines, Robert E. Lee had been Jefferson Davis's military advisor, not a commander. No one realized how brilliant he would be as leader of the Confederate forces.

The End of the Peninsula Campaign

After Malvern Hill, McClellan's commanders pushed him to attack Lee. They thought the Confederates could be beaten, but McClellan refused.

McClellan had given up, even though he was in a good position to win. He might have ended the war if he had attacked, but he still thought he would lose without reinforcements. By September 3, 1862, he and his troops were back in Washington, DC.

Lee wanted to continue his attacks and destroy the Union army. He knew, though, that he could not. He had lost 20,000 men, almost one-quarter of his force. Still, Lee had won a strategic victory. Richmond had not fallen and the North was on the run. To the South, he was a hero. They thought he had turned the tide for the Confederacy.

In the North, people were unhappy. They had hoped the Peninsula Campaign would end the war. Instead, it seemed like it would last longer and be even bloodier. Although the Union had won important victories in the West, it seemed to be losing the war in the East.

The Battle of Malvern Hill was fought July 1, 1862. It was the final battle of the Peninsula Campaign.

Second Battle of Manassas

I t did not look good for the Union army after the Peninsula Campaign. Many Americans thought the South was winning the war. Even though Union troops had important victories in the West, this did not help public opinion.

Northerners were worried because they thought their side should win easily. Southerners felt new pride and strength in their army's successes. In Europe, England and France waited for Confederate victories. They would only support the new nation if they thought it could survive.

After the Peninsula Campaign

On the peninsula, General McClellan kept his troops near the warships on the James River. Even though he had led the Union to victory at Malvern Hill, McClellan would not attack Robert E. Lee's army. He still thought he needed more troops and supplies. As he waited, Confederate and Union armies continued to skirmish for six more weeks. Neither side was ready to make the next big move.

General Lee's Strategy

General Lee worked on his new battle strategy. He would not wait for the North to attack. Instead, he wanted to force Northern troops out of the South. He did not have as many men or supplies as the North.

Major Events

1862

July 12–29
Pope's combined forces gather in Culpeper Courthouse

August 9
Jackson attacks in Cedar Mountain

August 14
McClellan withdraws from Peninsula to join Pope

August 15
Lee's army unites in Gordonsville

August 27
Jackson destroys the Union supply depot in Manassas

August 28–30
The Second Battle of Manassas

He discovered he could win by using his smaller size as an advantage, quickly moving his men in ways that the Union army did not expect.

Lincoln Changes Commanders

Lincoln was very disappointed with McClellan. He **demoted** McClellan and appointed Henry Halleck General-in-Chief. Halleck was now in command of all the Union armies. McClellan remained in charge of the Army of the Potomac, but now he reported to General Halleck.

GENERAL JOHN POPE Lincoln also brought in General John Pope to take control of the reorganized Army of Virginia. Pope had made a name for himself in the Western Theater. Lincoln wanted him to form one large force from the three smaller armies that fought in Virginia.

POPE'S PLANS Unlike McClellan, Pope was ready to fight. Unfortunately, he was also a loudmouth who bragged a lot. McClellan and many other Union leaders and soldiers did not like or respect him. Southerners also disliked him because of the way he treated **civilians**. Pope and his men took food and supplies from Virginia farmers. He threatened to arrest or hang anyone who helped the Confederacy. General Lee had a very strong desire to put an end to Pope and his ideas.

General John Pope took command of the Army of Virginia.

> " *If General McClellan does not want to use the army, I would like to borrow it for a time.* "
>
> —Abraham Lincoln, January 10, 1862

The Fight Moves North

Pope planned to capture an important Confederate railroad center in Gordonsville. He wanted to cut off supplies that went through there to Richmond. Between July 12 and July 29, he gathered about 40,000 Union troops in Culpeper Courthouse, 30 miles (48 km) north of Gordonsville.

The Battle of Cedar Mountain

Lee knew he had to hold off this new threat. He decided to split his army in half and send Stonewall Jackson and 24,000 men to Gordonsville.

On August 9, Jackson's army had its first battle at Cedar Mountain, about 20 miles (32 km) north of Gordonsville. The Confederates defeated the smaller Union force, but pulled back when more Union troops arrived.

> " *I don't like Jackson's movements—he will suddenly appear when least expected.* "
>
> —General George McClellan, telegram to Major General Henry Halleck, August 14, 1862

The Forces Gather

On August 3, Halleck ordered McClellan to leave the peninsula. Halleck wanted to combine McClellan's troops with Pope's. McClellan did not want to return to Washington, but he had no choice. On August 14, he finally began to move his army. McClellan decided they would travel by water. This delayed his joining Pope and his forces.

Lee wasted no time. With McClellan gone, Richmond was not in as much danger. However, Pope's army was not that far away. Lee also knew the Union forces would soon be much larger than the Confederate's. So Lee decided to attack Pope before McClellan could arrive with reinforcements.

By August 15, Lee had moved most of his army to Gordonsville. Once again, he used the railroad to travel quickly. Both sides now had about 55,000 men. For ten days, they fought small skirmishes. Pope withdrew his army further north to a safer position.

Looking for Stonewall Jackson

Pope's army was too big for Lee to attack directly, but he could not wait much longer. McClellan's army would be arriving. Lee decided to use Stonewall Jackson once again.

Treasure at the Manassas Depot

Lee could not attack Pope from the front, but he knew Pope would not expect to be attacked from behind. Pope's army was between Lee's force and the Union supply **depot** in Manassas. Lee would cause a lot of damage if his men cut off Pope's supply line from Washington.

Once again, Jackson and his men marched with incredible speed. In only two days, they circled 56 miles around Pope's troops to reach the depot. The train cars there were filled with supplies. Besides ammunition

People in the War

Clara Barton

Clara Barton wanted to help the troops. At first, she brought soldiers treats such as soap and tobacco. But when she saw the war's terrible casualties, she became a nurse. She often helped doctors right on the battlefield. At Cedar Mountain and Second Manassas, she cared for the wounded. After the war, she started the American Red Cross.

and uniforms, they carried food. The Confederate soldiers were starving and ragged. They ate candy, oranges, and canned foods. They took everything they could carry and burned the rest.

Pope Guesses Wrong

Jackson and his 25,000 men moved back to a position near the old Manassas battleground. They expected to be joined by the rest of the Confederate army soon. Pope had the opposite idea. He thought that Jackson was going to join the rest of Lee's forces back in Gordonsville.

Pope wanted to stop Jackson's smaller unit before the Confederates were able to combine forces. He sent his troops out to find Jackson. They were scattered around the area. Pope did not realize the rest of the Confederate army was marching toward him. He was not prepared for a larger battle.

Return to Manassas

On the evening of August 28, a Union brigade finally found Jackson in an area called Stony Ridge. It overlooked the battlefield where the two enemies fought just over a year before.

Pope prepared to attack Jackson the next day. He thought Jackson was trapped. Jackson, though, had deliberately revealed his hiding place. He wanted to distract the Union commanders so they did not realize that Lee and the rest of the Confederate army were nearby.

On August 29, Pope attacked, but he was surprised to find a stronger Confederate army than he expected. The fighting was fierce. Jackson's men were in a good defensive position. When they ran out of ammunition, they threw rocks at the Union soldiers.

Union soldiers also fought hard and bravely. On August 30, Pope tried attacking again. Lee was ready for him with fresh troops. Both sides gained and lost ground throughout the day. Finally, at 6:00 P.M. that evening, Pope retreated back toward Washington.

> *Lee has arrived, and our hopes are high that we will wipe them clean out this time…. [Lee] is silent, inscrutable, strong, like a god.*
>
> —Lieutenant John H. Camberlayne, August 15, 1862

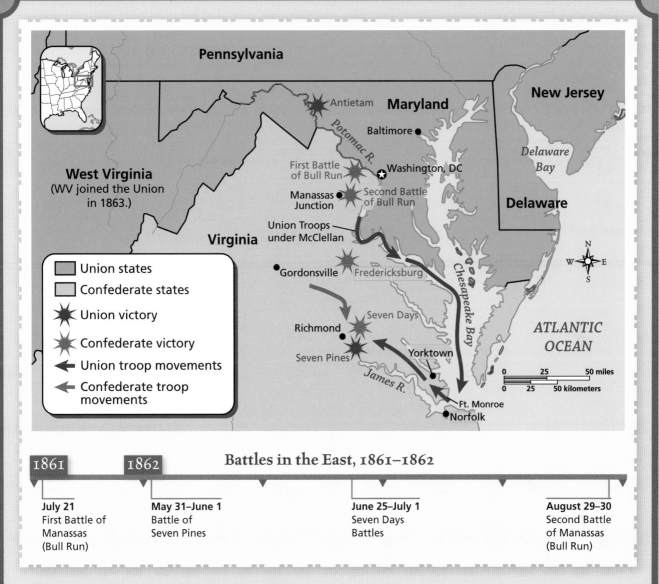

Battles in the East, 1861–1862

1861

1862

July 21
First Battle of
Manassas
(Bull Run)

May 31–June 1
Battle of
Seven Pines

June 25–July 1
Seven Days
Battles

August 29–30
Second Battle
of Manassas
(Bull Run)

The Results of the Battle

Five days of battles resulted in about 25,000 casualties. This was five times more than the number of men who had been killed, wounded, and missing at the first Battle of Manassas.

Once again, Lincoln had to deal with generals who failed. He sent Pope west to Minnesota. Lincoln still did not have a commander that he trusted. McClellan had been of little help at Manassas, even though his troops arrived in time to fight. The president knew, though, that the soldiers loved their general. Lincoln had doubts, but he made McClellan commander of the eastern forces for a second time.

Once again, the South celebrated. Only a few months before, Union troops had been 6 miles (10 km) from Richmond. Now Confederate troops were only 20 miles (32 km) from Washington, DC. Lee had fought a brave and smart war. His men were ragged and fought against great odds, but their courage and passion kept them going.

The Civil War Begins

When the first shots were fired on Fort Sumter in April 1861, many Americans did not have strong loyalties to either side. People thought the war would end quickly. They were sure the more powerful Union would crush the Confederates. However, poor Northern commanders and daring Southern strategies kept the war going. Soon the country was in a bloody conflict with no end in sight.

By August 1862, many citizens were touched by the deaths and hardships of the war. Fear and anger had hardened people on both sides. The wounds between North and South were so deep that many did not heal. To this day, memories of the Civil War still affect feelings between Northern and Southern states.

Union troops in retreat after the Second Battle of Manassas.

GLOSSARY

abolitionist A person who argued for the end of slavery in the United States

arsenal A place where military arms and ammunition are stored

betray To act against one's country or friends

blockade To use hostile ships to close off trade

breadbasket An agricultural area that provides an important source of grain

cabinet The council of advisors that advises the President of the United States

campaign The military operations designed to accomplish a certain goal

casualties A loss in the fighting strength of a military unit due to causes such as wounds or death

civilian A person who is not a member of the military or involved in fighting

demoted To be moved down to a lower rank

depot An important location where food and supplies are kept

division A unit made up of about 12,000 men within an army during the Civil War

economy The overall money resources of a state, region, or nation

federal government The central government of a union of states

flank The right or left side of the position of a military force

fortify To strengthen

hostage A captured person who will not be released until certain demands are met

inaugural address A speech given by the President of the United States at a ceremony that marks the beginning of a term in office

legislature A governmental assembly of elected officials that can pass laws

mass graves A common place where large numbers of the dead are buried after battle

merchant ship An unarmed ship that takes passengers or cargo from one place to another

militia A unit of citizen soldiers often called upon during emergencies within a state

neutral An individual, state, or nation that chooses not to take sides in a war or political conflict

prominent A person who stands out from the crowd as a result of accomplishments or wealth or a thing that stands out due to its size or uniqueness

provisions Food and supplies

regiment A unit made up of about 1,000 men within the army during the Civil War

reinforcements Additional men who take the place of casualties or exhausted soldiers in battle

rights The personal freedoms or legal guarantees outlined by state or national laws

rotunda A dome-covered circular room

skirmish A brief conflict between troops

slavery When a person is owned by another in a condition of forced labor with little or no pay

sovereign nation An independent nation that has its own government, makes its own laws, and conducts its own affairs

strategy Plans for conducting warfare including the movement of armed forces in relation to an enemy

trenches Defensive works surrounding a military position with the purpose of helping to defend a military force against an enemy

unconditional surrender The complete surrender of a military force or individual

Union A group of states joined together under a common government; their relationship to that government is outlined in a constitution

uprising A revolt or the rising up of individuals to take a specific action

U.S. Constitution The document that contains the laws of the United States of America and provides the rules by which states and individuals relate to the federal government

U.S. Supreme Court The highest court in the United States; its decisions may overrule decisions by lower state or federal courts

volunteers People who willingly offer their services without any expectation of payment

MORE INFORMATION

Books

Bolotin, Norman. *Civil War A to Z: A Young Person's Guide to Over 100 People, Places, and Points of Importance.* Dutton Children's Books, 2002.

Elliot, Henry. *Frederick Douglass: From Slavery to Statesman.* Crabtree Publishing Company, 2010.

Goodheart, Adam. *1861: The Civil War Awakening.* New York: Alfred A. Knopf, 2011.

Herbert, Janis. *The Civil War for Kids: A History with 21 Activities* (For Kids series). Chicago Review Press, 1999.

Horn, Geoffrey M. *John Brown: Putting Actions Above Words.* Crabtree Publishing Company, 2010.

McPherson, James M. *The Illustrated Battle Cry of Freedom: The Civil War Era.* Oxford University Press, 2003.

Stanchak, John. *Eyewitness: Civil War.* Dorling Kindersley Publishing, 2000.

Ward, Geoffrey C. *The Civil War: An Illustrated History.* Alfred A. Knopf, 1992.

Websites

www.civilwar.org/education/students/kids websites.html
Civil War Trust Websites for Kids. Has articles, photos, a glossary of Civil War terms, lists of books, and links to other websites.

www.civil-war.net
The Civil War Home Page. Has a photo gallery, lists of books and movies, battle maps, articles, diary excerpts, and reference materials.

www.pbs.org/civilwar
The Civil War/PBS. Companion site to Ken Burns's DVD *The Civil War.* Includes photos, maps, and video clips.

http://memory.loc.gov/ammem/cwphtml/ cwphome.html
Library of Congress Civil War photographs

About the Author

Jane Gould is an educational writer who has written about many subjects for all grade levels, as well as for teachers. She is interested in presenting material in a way that captures students' imaginations, while giving them the important information they need.

INDEX